Bible Verse Coloring Book For Adults

Hope Winters

D1716290

Isaiah 40:31 (NIV)

Those who
hope
in
the
LORD

will renew their strength.
They will soar on wings like eagles;
they will run
and
not grow weary,
they will walk
and
not be faint
Isaiah 40:31

Proverbs 18:10 (NIV / ESV)

The name of the Lord is a strong tower;
The righteous run to it and are safe.

John 14:6 (NLT)

Isaiah 43:1 (ESV)

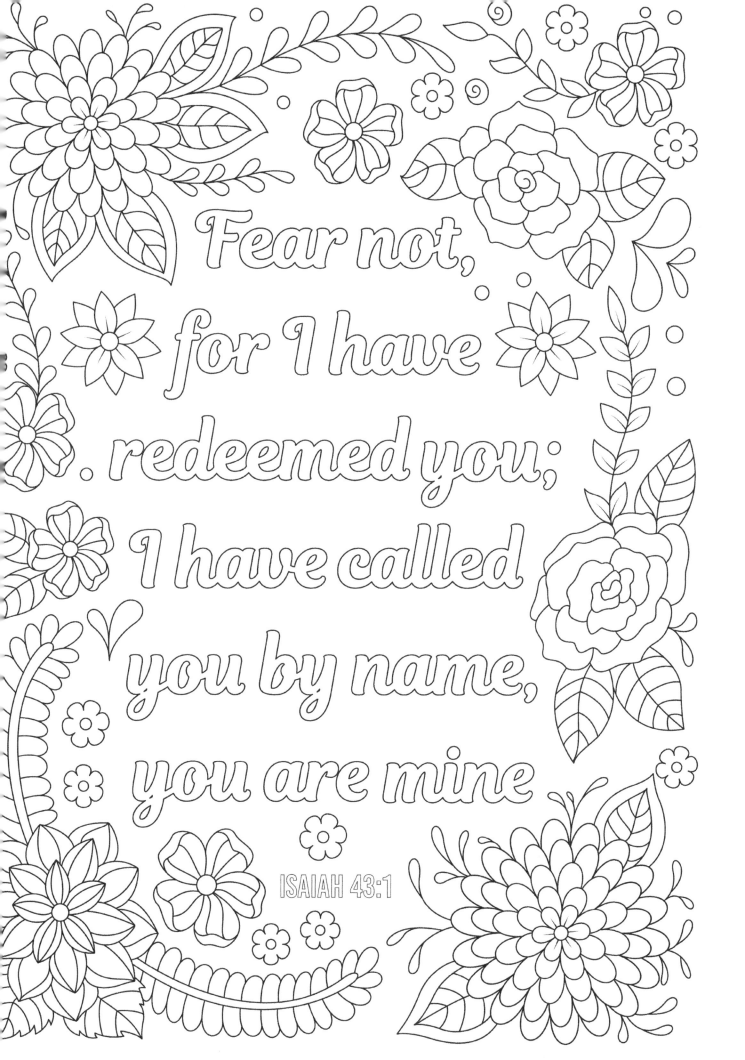

Fear not, for I have redeemed you; I have called you by name, you are mine

ISAIAH 43:1

1 Thessalonians 5:18 (WEB)

Mark 5:36 (NIV)

Lamentations 3:25 (NIV)

Psalm 19:1 (NIV)

The heavens declare the glory of God;
the skies proclaim the work of his hands

Luke 1:37 (NLT)

1 Peter 5:7 (NLT / NIV)

Give all your worries and cares to God; for He cares for you

Isaiah 43:1

Psalm 16:9

Psalm 4:7

You have filled my heart
with greater joy

Colossians 1:16-17

For all the things that were created

In Heaven and on Earth

visible and invisible

Whether or not thrones

or

rulers or authorities

All

things were

Created Through

Him and for

Him

Colossian 1:16-17

Psalm 46:10 (NIV)

Be still and know that
I am God

1 Peter 5:7 (NIV)

Psalm 51:10 (KJV)

2 Corinthians 5:17 (WEB)

If anyone is in Christ, he is a new creation; old things have passed away; all things have become new

Psalm 104:4

Based on Isaiah 41:10

Isaiah 26:1 (NIV)

We have
a strong city
He sets up walls
and Ramparts
for
Security

Based on Nehemiah 8:10 (NIV)

The JOY of the LORD is my strength

Based on John 1:12

Based on Psalm 28:7

the lord is my strength
and my shield,
in him my heart trusts

1 Peter 2:5 (NLT)

Psalm 118:24 (ESV)

Proverbs 31:25 (NLT)

She laughs
without
fear
of the
future

Proverbs 31:25

If you enjoyed this book,
you might also enjoy
Psalms Bible Coloring Book For Adults:
Scripture Verses To Encourage and Inspire As You Color
by the same author

Made in the USA
Monee, IL
23 November 2024

71005940R00033